Books are to be returned on or before
the last date below.

How Artists Use

Colour

Paul Flux

Heinemann
LIBRARY

H www.heinemann.co.uk
Visit our website to find out more information about Heinemann Library books.

To order:
☎ Phone 44 (0) 1865 888066
📄 Send a fax to 44 (0) 1865 314091
💻 Visit the Heinemann Bookshop at www.heinemann.co.uk to browse our catalogue and order online.

First published in Great Britain by Heinemann Library, Halley Court, Jordan Hill, Oxford OX2 8EJ, a division of Reed Educational and Professional Publishing Ltd.
Heinemann is a registered trademark of Reed Educational & Professional Publishing Ltd.

OXFORD MELBOURNE AUCKLAND JOHANNESBURG BLANTYRE
GABORONE IBADAN PORTSMOUTH (NH) USA CHICAGO

Designed by Celia Floyd
Illustrations by Jo Brooker/Ann Miller
Originated by Ambassador Litho Ltd.
Printed and bound in Hong Kong/China

05 04 03 02 01
10 9 8 7 6 5 4 3 2 1

ISBN 0 431 11520 6

British Library Cataloguing in Publication Data

Flux, Paul
  How artists use colour.
  1. Colour in art – Juvenile literature
  I. Title
  701.8'5

Acknowledgements
The Publishers would like to thank the following for permission to reproduce photographs:

© 2001 Mondrian/Holtzman Trust c/o Beeldrecht, Amsterdam, Holland & DACS, London: p20; AKG, London: pp7, 9, 14, 17, /© ADAGP, Paris and DACS, London 2001 p27, /© Munch Museum/Munch - Ellingsen Group, BONO, Oslo, DACS, London 2001 p19; Boomalli Aboriginal Artists. Purchased with the assistance of funds from National Gallery admission charges and commissioned in 1987. Collection: National Gallery of Australia, Canberra: p15; Bridgeman Art Library: /© ADAGP, Paris and DACS pp16, 18, /© Kate Rothko Prizel and Christopher Rothko/DACS 2001 p12, Peter Willi p11; Corbis/National Gallery, London: p28; SCALA: p10; Tate Gallery, London/© Succession H Matisse/DACS 2001: p13; Trevor Clifford/Jo Brooker: pp23, 24, 25.

Cover photograph reproduced with permission of Bridgeman Art Library.

Every effort has been made to contact copyright holders of any material reproduced in this book. Any omissions will be rectified in subsequent printings if notice is given to the Publisher.

Contents

Any words appearing in the text in bold, **like this**, are explained in the Glossary.

Making colours

How many different colours do you think there are? Our eyes can see thousands of colours, some bright, some of them dark. Red, yellow and blue are called **primary colours**. They cannot be made by mixing together other colours. Primary colours can be mixed to make every other colour.

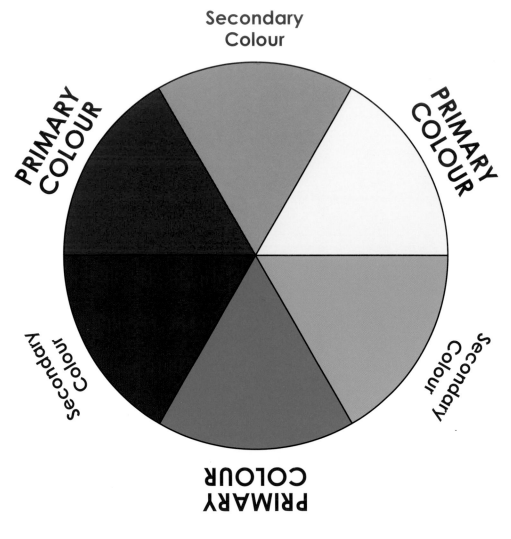

Secondary Colour

PRIMARY COLOUR

PRIMARY COLOUR

Secondary Colour

PRIMARY COLOUR

Secondary Colour

4

Secondary colours are made by mixing two primary colours together. By adding more of one colour you get different **shades**. If you mix all three primary colours together you get a muddy brown! Not all animals' eyes work in the same way as ours. Many see a world in which everything is colourless.

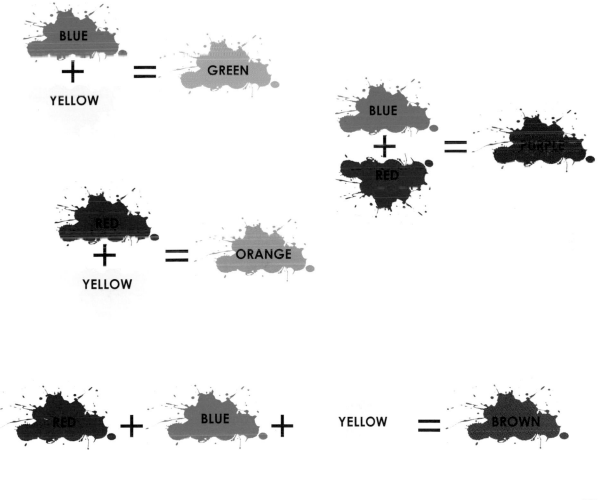

colour partners

Opposite colours on the colour wheel (see page 4) **complement** one another. This means that they work together so that they both stand out. Which red blob seems strongest to you? All three are exactly the same, but the one on the green background seems much brighter. Can you see how the purple and orange blobs both seem very bright because they are with their **complementary colour**?

Vincent van Gogh, *Portrait of the Postman Joseph Roulin,* 1889

Van Gogh is well known for his use of complementary colours. Look how the green background contrasts with the dark hat and coat, and the wavy beard, to make the face of the postman really stand out. The green eyes are strong and searching. Look at him for a while. Is he looking at you, or past you? What do you think is on his mind?

Warm and cool colours

Warm colours remind us of fire and sunshine. They are red, yellow and orange. Often artists use these colours to show strong feelings. The cool colours are blue and green. These make us think of the sky and the sea. When artists use cool colours their pictures can seem cold and lacking in feeling.

8

The French artist Paul Cézanne used warm colours to give his pictures great strength. Here he has placed fruit on a white cloth and surrounded it with **earth colours**. The warm colours bring the **scene** to life. They make the ordinary objects seem extra special. Have you ever seen apples look so dazzling?

Paul Cézanne, *Apples and Oranges*, 1895–1900

colour makes a difference!

Egyptian hieroglyphic writing

Colour can add meaning to many types of art. Look at these ancient Egyptian letters, which we call **hieroglyphs**. The walls of the tombs of kings were often covered with religious writing like this. The colours do not change any of the meaning, but the yellows, greens and browns make the writing more **decorative**. Can you make your own writing more interesting by using different colours?

Rose window, Notre Dame Cathedral, Paris, about 1250

Stained glass is found in churches and has been used for hundreds of years. This window was made more than 700 years ago. Light floods through the glass and fills the inside of the church with bright colours. People standing beneath this window can be covered with rainbow colours, which change as the light outside changes.

How artists use colour

Artists use colour in many ways. This painting is by an artist called Mark Rothko. He used big blocks of colour with fuzzy edges to show different moods and feelings. This kind of art is called **abstract**. It uses colour and shape, rather than people, places or objects, to make the picture. How does this painting make you feel?

Mark Rothko, *White Cloud Over Purple*, 1957

Henri Matisse made this picture when he was over 80 years old. His helpers painted large sheets of paper, and Matisse cut them into shapes and then stuck them onto **canvas**. He wanted to **explore** the difference between drawing objects, and using colour to show them in art. After it was finished Matisse called this picture *The Snail*. Can you see why?

Henri Matisse, *The Snail*, 1953

colour adds meaning

Fra Angelico, *The Annunciation*, 1437–45

This painting is on the wall of a **monastery** in Florence, in Italy. The angel Gabriel is kneeling in front of Mary to tell her that she will give birth to Jesus, the Son of God. Look closely at Gabriel's wings. The blue and orange feathers **complement** one other, and so do the red clothes and green grass. Here colour is being used to help express deep religious feelings.

14

Around 200 years ago, people from Europe discovered Australia and moved there. In 1988 many Australians celebrated this event. The **Aborigines** had mixed feelings because settlers had taken much of their land. A group of 43 artists made this forest of hollow log bone-coffins, some over 3 metres tall. The natural **earth colours** and ancient **designs** celebrate the Aboriginal culture.

Ramingining Artists, *The Aboriginal Memorial,* **1987–88**

colours in balance

The French artist Claude Monet was interested in the effect of light on everyday **scenes**. He painted many pictures of the same places at different times of the day. In this beautiful painting he has balanced the blue light of early evening in winter, with an orange sky. Can you sense the stillness? The colours **combine** to create a feeling of great peace.

Claude Monet, *Haystacks: Snow Effect*, 1891

Caspar David Friedrich, *The Monk by the Sea*, 1808–10

Many paintings work well when the colours are used in balance. Here we can see a cloudy sky reflected onto a bare cliff top. The blue **tones** weave together to create a feeling of enormous space. The lone man gazing into the distance seems so small, set against the huge sky. What would you think about if you were standing there?

Colours that Shout!

Joan Miró, *Figures in the Night*, 1960

Colours can be used in ways which surprise us. In this picture, dark night-time shapes are surrounded by strong splashes of colour which seem to leap off the **canvas**. But these bright **tones** are held in check by a mysterious darkness. Think about the title of the painting. Would you want to be alone on a night like this?

18

Edvard Munch, *The Scream*, 1893

Bold colours are used again here, to give the painting its strength. Swirling **shades** of red and orange push out from the canvas. Is the figure a man or a woman? Notice how the bright colours add to the excitement of the painting. Do you think the scream is one of terror, or excitement?

Colour and the modern world

This was one of Piet Mondrian's last paintings. All his life he **experimented** with the **primary colours**. He painted **abstract** pictures using yellow, red and blue. He also used grey and white blocks, and black lines to separate them. The straight lines of New York city's streets gave Mondrian the idea for this painting. The colours look like flags waving at a parade.

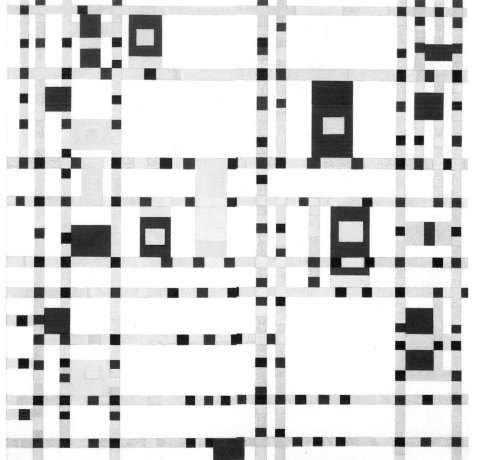

Piet Mondrian,
Broadway Boogie Woogie,
1942–43

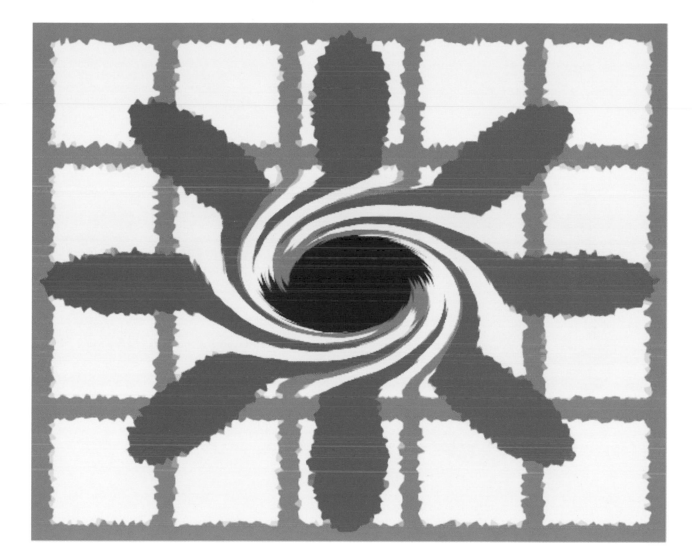

Today we can use computers to make great pictures. Colours, lines and shapes can all be changed very quickly and you can repeat patterns easily. If you have a good printer the results can be very exciting. You can even use the computer to send your picture to a friend in another country!

Mixing colours

How many colours are there? 10? 20? 100? 1000? More?
Start with one of the **primary colours** and **experiment** by
adding different colours to it. Keep a record of which
colours you have mixed and the new colours you make.
Use the different **shades** you have made to paint
something simple like the sky, or water.

22

Collect lots of see-through coloured sweet wrappers.
Tape some of the wrappers to a window and **overlap**
them to make different colours. Make as many different
colours as you can. Fold the wrappers in half if you want
to make a colour stronger. Can you make a simple
picture like the one above?

When colours move, our eyes can see things which are not there. Spinning colours can have a strange effect. Make some simple spinners and decorate them. Use the **designs** shown here to help you. Which **combinations** of colour work best? What happens when you only use two **primary colours**? What happens with the spinners that are just black and white?

24

How to make a spinner

1. Cut out a circle of card about 15 cm wide and ask an adult to make two holes about 1 cm from the centre.
2. Draw a design on one side and then colour it. Repeat the design on the other side but colour it differently.
3. Get some thin string or wool and thread it through the two holes. Knot the string to make a loop.

Hold the string in both hands, twist it and then gently pull. The card will spin and you will see the colours change.

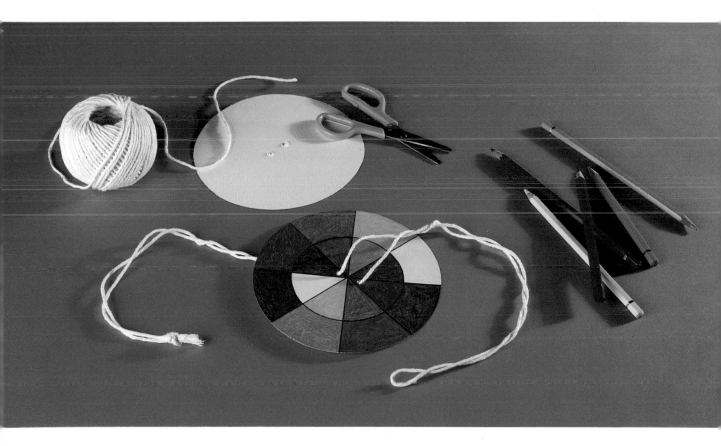

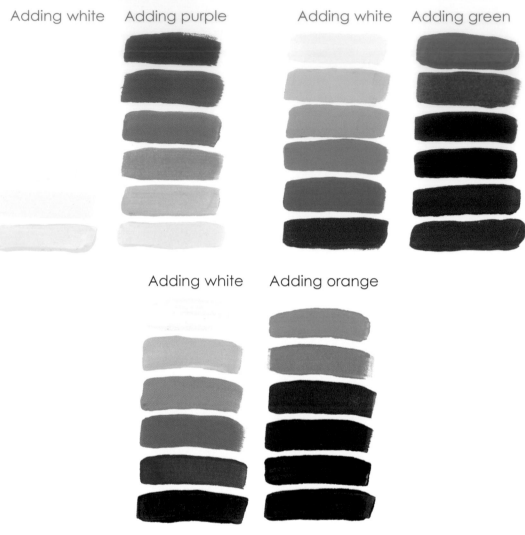

Adding white   Adding purple   Adding white   Adding green

Adding white   Adding orange

Put two big blobs of one of the **primary colours** onto a **palette**. To one blob gradually add white, to the other add tiny amounts of the **complementary colour**. As you discover different **shades** make your own **tone** ladders like the ones above. Tones that match each other on the ladders often work best together.

26

Here Claude Monet has used the light and dark tones of purple, blue and green to paint his lily pond. The delicate colouring suggests that the time is early morning or evening. Monet was interested in the way light and water **interacted** to continually change the **scene**. He eventually painted his lily pond many times, and each picture is different.

Claude Monet, *Waterlilies*, 1907

Painting with dots

Georges Pierre Seurat, *Bathers at Asnieres*, 1883–84

Georges Seurat was an artist who **experimented** with colour in a **scientific** way. He did not paint with **brush strokes**, but used tiny dots of colour instead. Look at the boy to the right of the picture. He seems surrounded with bright light. Seurat used light and dark **tones** and mixed them together to create this special effect.

Seurat's way of painting tricks us into seeing colours. The colours do not blend together on the **canvas**, but inside our heads! Try experimenting with tiny dots of colour. How can you make them lighter or darker? Which colours work well together? Make a simple picture just using dots of colour – it is not as easy as it first looks!

Glossary

Aborigine native person of Australia

abstract kind of art which does not try to show people or things, but instead uses shape and colour to make the picture

brush strokes marks in paint made by a brush

canvas strong woven material on which many artists paint

combination two or more things together

complement to make another colour seem bright

complementary colour a colour opposite another on the colour wheel

decorative pleasant or interesting to look at

design lines and shapes which decorate art

earth colour warm colour found in nature, such as brown or red

experiment to try things out, or repeat something until you like the result

explore to examine how something works

hieroglyph symbol used by the ancient Egyptians in picture writing

interact how things work with each other

monastery building where monks live and pray

overlap partly cover

palette board used to mix colours on

primary colour red, blue and yellow – colours which
  cannot be made by mixing other colours

secondary colour a colour which is made by mixing two
  primary colours together

scene view painted by an artist

scientific like science, testing ideas in an ordered way

shade a darker or lighter version of a colour

stained glass small pieces of coloured glass put
  together to make a picture

tone shades and depth of colour, from light to dark or
  dull to bright

Index

Titles in the *How Artists Use* series include:

Hardback   0 431 11520 6

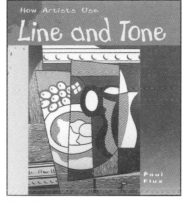

Hardback   0 431 11524 9

Hardback   0 431 11522 2

Hardback   0 431 11523 0

Hardback   0 431 11521 4

Find out about other Heinemann books on our website www.heinemann.co.uk/library